To my thirty-seven chicks—my nieces
and nephews—and all others:
Don't forget to live your dreams.

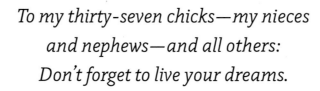

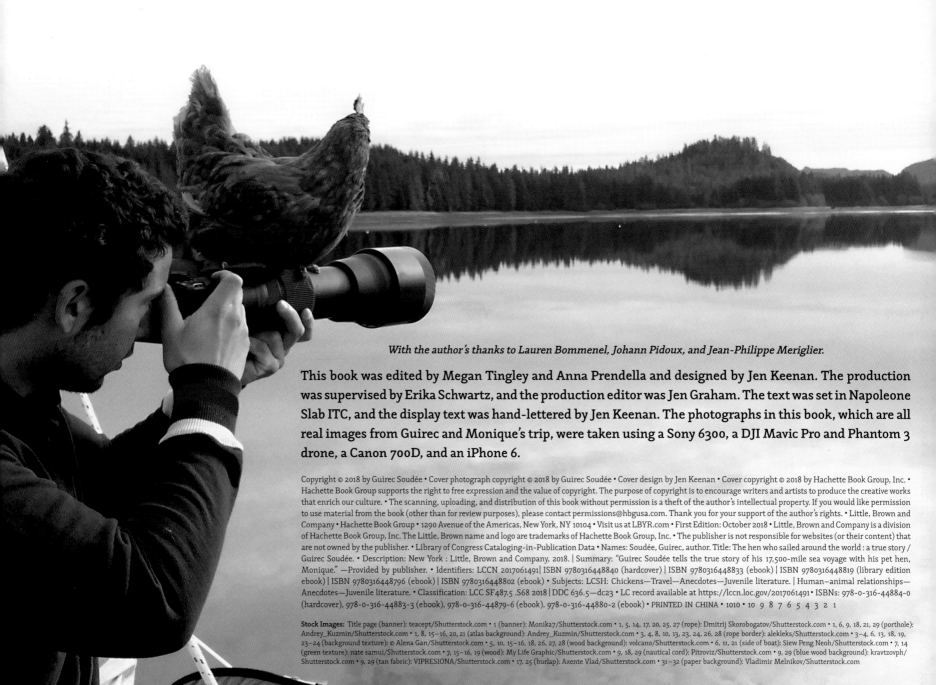

With the author's thanks to Lauren Bommenel, Johann Pidoux, and Jean-Philippe Meriglier.

This book was edited by Megan Tingley and Anna Prendella and designed by Jen Keenan. The production was supervised by Erika Schwartz, and the production editor was Jen Graham. The text was set in Napoleone Slab ITC, and the display text was hand-lettered by Jen Keenan. The photographs in this book, which are all real images from Guirec and Monique's trip, were taken using a Sony 6300, a DJI Mavic Pro and Phantom 3 drone, a Canon 700D, and an iPhone 6.

THE HEN WHO SAILED AROUND THE WORLD

A True Story

By Guirec Soudée

L B

LITTLE, BROWN AND COMPANY
NEW YORK   BOSTON

When I decided to set off from France on my around-the-world adventure, everyone told me I couldn't bring a hen. "She'll just make trouble," they said. "She'll hate the sea too much to lay eggs." And then I met Monique. She laid an egg her very first night on board! She loves the ocean, and so do I.

Monique immediately begins following me everywhere. She is so curious about me, our ship, and our upcoming adventure, although she is not a very skilled navigator yet.

My brave hen loves being outside on the ocean most of all. Every morning she sings to tell me she is awake, and then on the deck she catches flying fish in her beak!

After much preparation in Saint Barthélemy in the West Indies, we set off for Greenland, where we will try to be the youngest navigator and first chicken ever to cross the dangerous Northwest Passage over Canada.

It is just us and the ocean, and we are flying! Whether I am raising the sail or keeping a lookout, Monique is always trying to help out (although she is not in fact very helpful).

We listen to a lot of music while working. Sometimes Monique doesn't like the song, and she turns her head fast at me to say, "Guirec! Are you serious?" Then I must change the song right away.

Every time I catch a fish, Monique jumps on it to eat it first. If it were up to her, I would have nothing to eat but eggs. When I feed Monique, she is so happy, she sings with all her heart. That is the best song of all.

Monique has two houses, one inside and one outside, but she doesn't spend any time in them. She is simply not happy unless she is helping me sail. And I will need her help for the challenges ahead!

From here on out, the waters will be very dangerous.
Huge waves crash around our little boat, but together,
we are not afraid.

Then we see it—our first iceberg! Thrilled, we capture the moment with my special drone camera.

Of course, while I am taking our "brave adventurers" photo, Monique poops on my shoulder. I am so upset with her, and she just sings.

I didn't know if Monique would like paddleboarding, but this
adventurous hen cannot stand to be left behind—and her board
is even cooler than mine!

Neither of us has ever seen ice like this before! Monique is not afraid of anything.

Every morning, I have to cut the ice down to prevent it from sinking the boat. Monique is no help!

Soon, the ice freezes us in. We must wait out the ice, which is called "overwintering." We will be frozen in for four months. And yet, it is impossible to be afraid: The unknown is so beautiful.

Even when the boat is stuck, Monique will not be stopped!
She loves to stretch her legs and explore.

Since Monique will not stay on the boat, I sacrifice two of my
gloves to make her a sweater to keep her warm on her adventures.

What do you think I eat for these four months of ice? Eggs, of course!
And for Monique, we have over one hundred pounds of seeds. I hide
dried insects in her food for special treats.

The most curious hen you've ever met, my first mate explores both outside and inside. There is no one else for miles, but it's not a problem—Monique is very talkative. Her company and her eggs both save me during this long winter.

At last, after 130 days, the ice begins to crack
and split! We are free!

Monique and I meet many amazing friends in the Arctic. We escort a deer on her swim to protect her from sea lions, and we respectfully greet a polar bear.

Monique parades proudly for these husky puppies:
the first chicken they have ever seen.

Finally, one day Monique and I look at each other, and we decide it is time for this brave crew to sail home.

Of course, before we depart, we must patch up the boat. Monique helps by finding all the holes. Bosco the dog briefly joins the crew! He is a little troublemaker, and sometimes Monique pricks him with her beak to say, "Hey, calm down."

We did it! We are the youngest navigator and first chicken ever to sail the Northwest Passage.

We friends have sailed over 17,500 miles together in this wild, majestic landscape, silent but for Monique's singing, and we will always remember it.

To be honest, it is hard to say goodbye to the adventure. Monique and I are so blissful on the ocean together. It is time to rest, but we know in our hearts that soon we will be back. Where will our next journey take us?

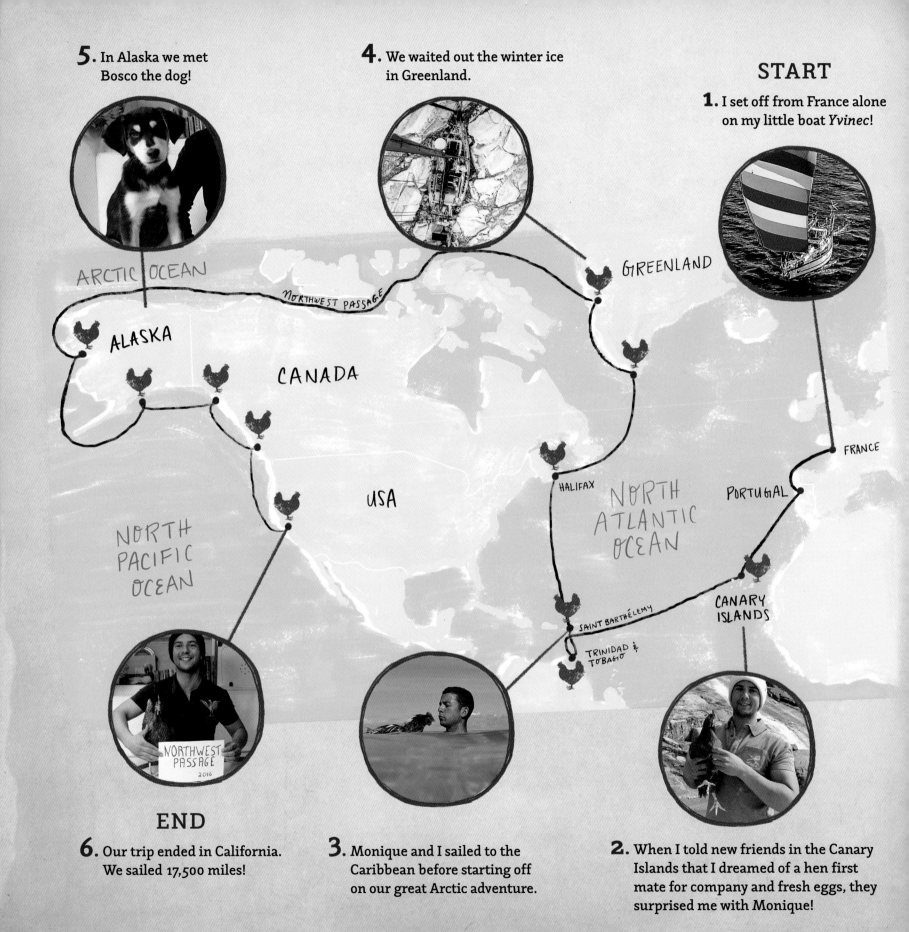

5. In Alaska we met Bosco the dog!

4. We waited out the winter ice in Greenland.

START

1. I set off from France alone on my little boat *Yvinec*!

ARCTIC OCEAN

NORTHWEST PASSAGE

GREENLAND

ALASKA

CANADA

FRANCE

HALIFAX

NORTH ATLANTIC OCEAN

PORTUGAL

USA

NORTH PACIFIC OCEAN

SAINT BARTHÉLEMY

TRINIDAD & TOBAGO

CANARY ISLANDS

NORTHWEST PASSAGE 2016

END

6. Our trip ended in California. We sailed 17,500 miles!

3. Monique and I sailed to the Caribbean before starting off on our great Arctic adventure.

2. When I told new friends in the Canary Islands that I dreamed of a hen first mate for company and fresh eggs, they surprised me with Monique!

We became the youngest solo sailor and first chicken ever to sail the treacherous Northwest Passage over Canada!

The whole journey took about 1,300 days—over 3 and a half years—because we made so many long stops to meet and learn from new friends.

I caught many fish: tuna, sea bream, halibut, cod, salmon, and a barracuda (which I had to throw back because I did not have a fridge, and it was too large to eat!), as well as lobsters, crabs, shrimp, and a bunch of sea urchins by accident—not to mention the hundreds of flying fish that flew on board for Monique to catch.

Over the course of the adventure, Monique laid 1,040 eggs!